T0195972

doodle
noodle

written by kate seng & illustrated by cat kahnle

To my Mom, Alice, for always encouraging me and to
Brian, Jackson, Graham and Chloe for being my inspiration.

Archway Publishing books may be ordered through booksellers or by contacting:

Archway Publishing
1663 Liberty Drive
Bloomington, IN 47403
www.archwaypublishing.com
844-669-3957

ISBN: 978-1-6657-0271-3 (sc)
ISBN: 978-1-6657-0657-5 (hc)
ISBN: 978-1-6657-0270-6 (e)

Print information available on the last page.

Archway Publishing rev. date: 05/04/2021

ANN WALCZAK, is a Nashville-based writer and editor.
Originally from Cleveland, Ohio, she holds a BA in performing Arts,
and is a former hospitality manager and consultant

where is noodle?

Mazie collapsed to the ground. Where's Noodle?
She picked a flower and smelled it.

Mazie asked, "Where is my

SUPER
POOCH?"

Maybe I should ask the policeman from school. He always answers my questions, like "Why do you wear blue?" and "Why do you have a big

SHINY

badge?" Maybe someone can doodle Noodle! Who can doodle Noodle?, she thought.

I know, Rosa can doodle Noodle. Rosa makes

AMAZING

birthday cakes at the grocery store.
She makes the most beautiful flowers.

Maybe, thought Mazie, she can make a big cake with Noodle on the front.

Rosa can make flowers just like the ones on Noodle's collar.

Or, maybe Ms. Gayle, the painter from my art party, can doodle Noodle. She is so

TALL

I may need to ask mom to make the request. She might not hear me from way down low.

She painted the most

BEAUTIFUL

angel at my birthday party. It was glowing blue, yellow, and green!
Yes! She can doodle Noodle!

Jinny, the artist, can doodle Noodle.
Jinny wears colorful silk scarves in
her hair and has long,

FEATHERY

earrings. She has the loveliest skirts with
ruffles around the bottom.

Jinny makes sketches at the fair. She made my brother's head look like a big balloon with bug eyes. He was so

SMILEY,

I thought he might burst!

Matteo can doodle Noodle! Matteo created the bright blue mosaic in Mezzaluna, my favorite restaurant. He put all the pieces together like a jigsaw. I think someone called it

STARRY

night. Matteo can doodle Noodle at Mezzaluna, right on the wall. Everyone would see Noodle and she would come home again.

Mazie was starting to fret. Where is Noodle?
She never misses her afternoon walk.

She never leaves my side for this long. She likes the way
I pet her fur. I pet her even when my dad says she's

STINKY.

I don't mind. It's not like she smells as bad as my brother's
socks after soccer. Then I wouldn't want to pet him!

Come to think of it,

I CAN'T FIND
DAD EITHER!

Do I need someone to doodle dad, too?

That's when I heard it, the humming sound that mom's car makes when she rounds the corner. But, it wasn't mom. It was dad and Noodle!

I ran up to pet her fluffy fur. She didn't even smell. Actually, she smelled really

DELICIOUS,

like lilac and vanilla. Yummy!

She wasn't missing.
She was at the groomer!
Maybe I will doodle
beautifully groomed Noodle
and hang her on the fridge.

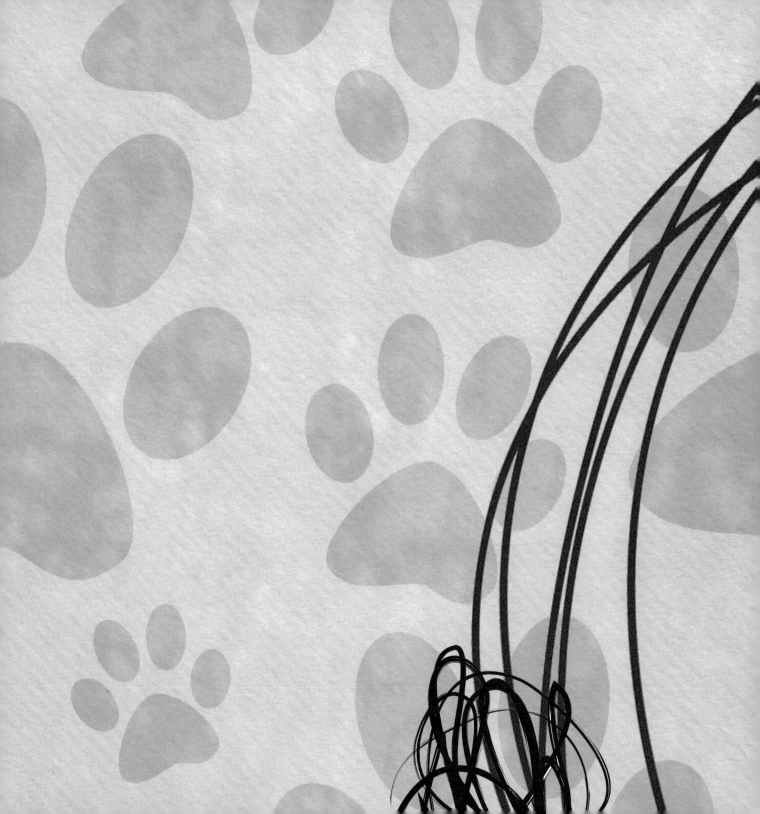

Printed in the United States
by Baker & Taylor Publisher Services